What's Up There?

Questions and Answers About Stars and Space

by DINAH MOCHÉ

Photographs, and Drawings by Tom Huffman

SCHOLASTIC INC.
New York Toronto London Auckland Sydney Tokyo

To Rebecca and Elizabeth who helped me, and to Mark, James, and Leonard, and all other boys and girls, who ask questions about stars.

The author wishes to thank Mr. George Lovi, Astronomer, The Vanderbilt Planetarium, Centerport, New York, for the Venus data on p. 31.

Cover photo: Copyright by the California Institute of Technology and Carnegie Institution of Washington. Reproduced by permission of the Hale Observatories.

Photo credits: *Hale Observatories, pp. 4, 6-7, 10, 42-43, 44, 46, 47, 52, 55, 57, 63; U.S. Naval Observatory, p. 18; NASA, pp. 29, 31, 33, 34; Museum of Natural History, New York, p. 41; Ted Shoemaker, p. 51.*

ISBN 0-590-04850-3

Text copyright © 1975 by Dinah L. Moché. Illustrations copyright © 1975 by Scholastic Inc. All rights reserved. Published by Scholastic Inc.

18 17 16 15 14 13 12 11 10   7 8 9/8

Contents

Dear Reader:

 If you go outside on a clear night and look up at the sky, you can see many, many stars. They are there for you to watch no matter where you live. As you look at the sky, you may ask:

 What is a star?

 How far away are the stars?

 Are there any creatures living someplace out in space?

 This book answers these questions — and many more — about stars and space, the moon and the sun, the planets and the universe. You may have asked some of these questions yourself.

The Author

A cluster of stars called The Pleiades
photographed through a large telescope.

Looking at the Stars

What is a star?

A star looks like a bright pinpoint of light in the night sky. It is really a gigantic hot ball of whirling gases, racing through space.

The star we know best is our hot blazing sun. It is only 93 million miles away from Earth.

The stars we see as pinpoints of light are *trillions* of miles away.

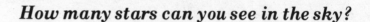

How many stars can you see in the sky?

If you are in a place where the sky is clear, and it is really dark at night — in the country or in the desert or at the seashore — you will be able to see about 2,000 stars with your naked eye. Scientists, using powerful telescopes, can see millions of stars in just one small part of the sky.

If you are in a big town or city the bright lights and tall buildings will blot out most of the stars. Then you will be able to see only the brightest stars in the sky.

Masses of luminous gas (called prominences) rising thousands of miles off the surface of the sun.

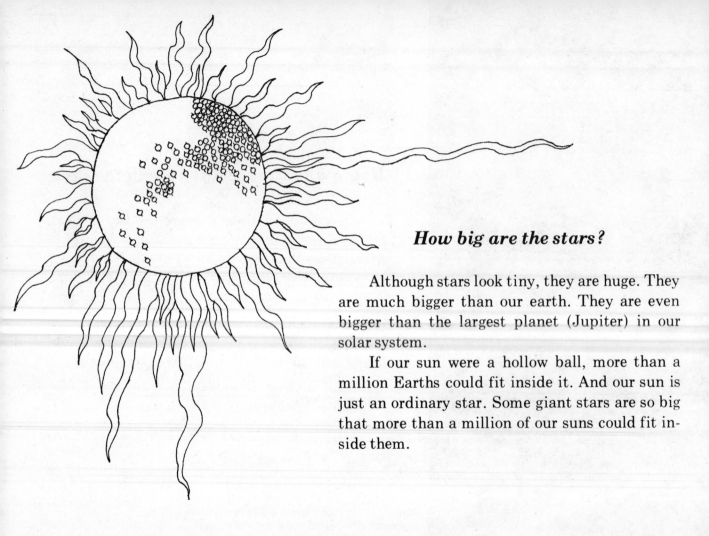

How big are the stars?

Although stars look tiny, they are huge. They are much bigger than our earth. They are even bigger than the largest planet (Jupiter) in our solar system.

If our sun were a hollow ball, more than a million Earths could fit inside it. And our sun is just an ordinary star. Some giant stars are so big that more than a million of our suns could fit inside them.

How far away are the stars?

Most stars are trillions of miles away. The closest star that can ever be seen at night is Alpha Centauri. It is about 25 trillion miles away from Earth. All the other stars are even farther away. Some stars are so far away that you couldn't see them even with the most powerful telescope.

If you could travel at the speed of light (186,000 miles per *second*), it would take you more than four years to get to Alpha Centauri.

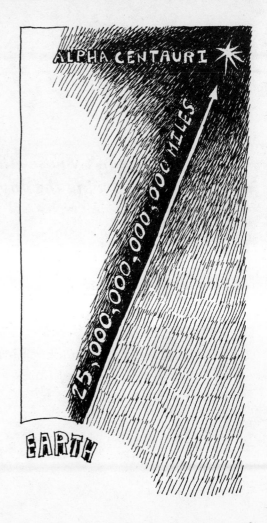

Why can't you see the stars during the day?

One star — our sun — is so close and so bright that it outshines all the other stars.

But if you ever have a chance to see a total eclipse of the sun — on a clear day — then you will be able to see stars in the daytime sky.

At a total solar eclipse, the moon moves in front of the sun. This makes Earth's daytime sky dark enough for a few minutes so that some stars can be seen.

A photograph of a total eclipse of the sun.

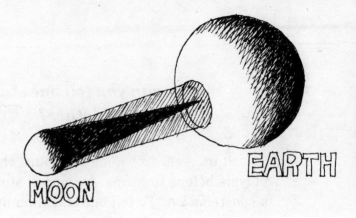

SUN

MOON

EARTH

Coming total solar eclipses

When	Where
July 31, 1981	Siberia
June 11, 1983	Indonesia
Nov. 22, 1984	Indonesia, South America
March 29, 1987	Central Africa
March 18, 1988	Philippines, Indonesia
July 22, 1990	Finland, Arctic regions

How can you tell one star from another?

Stars seem to belong to groups the way ball players belong to teams. A group of stars is called a *constellation*. To tell one star from another you can learn about the different constellations. One of the most famous constellations in the Northern Hemisphere is Ursa Major (the Big Bear). In this constellation you will find the Big Dipper.

People in ancient times named the constellations, and we still use the same names today. Those people imagined that the star groups were shaped like the heroes in their myths — Hercules or Orion. Or looked like a harp (Lyra) or a crown (Corona Borealis), or a lion (Leo) or a wolf (Lupus) or a bear (Ursa Major). The Big Dipper got its name because some people imagined that it looked like a huge dipper in the sky.

FIND THE BIG DIPPER

Is the sky always the same?

No. The sky is always changing. As our earth turns around (once a day) the stars appear to move across the sky.

It is as though you were sitting on a giant merry-go-round watching buildings and signs go by and then reappear.

And as our earth travels around the sun (once a year) different constellations appear in the sky. The sky in the winter is not the same as the sky in the summer or the sky in the fall or the spring.

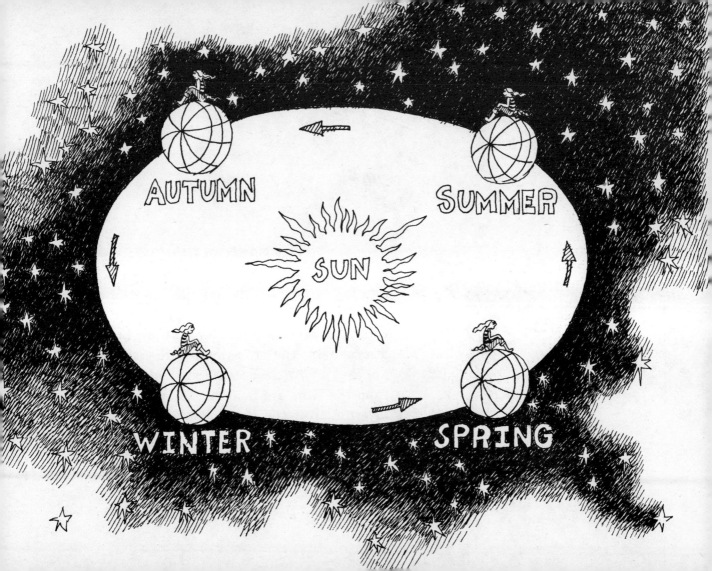

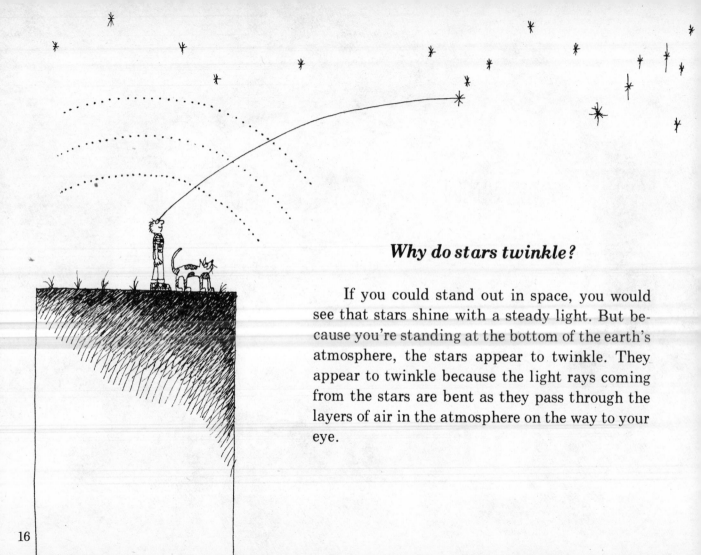

Why do stars twinkle?

If you could stand out in space, you would see that stars shine with a steady light. But because you're standing at the bottom of the earth's atmosphere, the stars appear to twinkle. They appear to twinkle because the light rays coming from the stars are bent as they pass through the layers of air in the atmosphere on the way to your eye.

Are all stars the same color?

No. There are different-colored stars in the sky. If you look very carefully you may see red, orange, yellow, and blue-white stars. The color of a star is caused by its temperature. All stars are very, very hot. But some stars are much hotter than others.

Blue stars are the hottest. Their surface temperature is over 19,000°F. Yellow stars — like our sun — are medium-hot stars. The red stars are the coolest. They are about 5500°F on the surface.

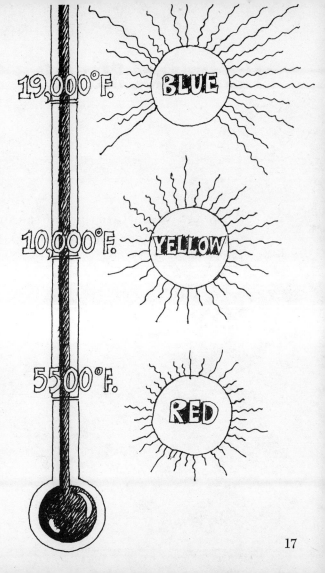

The Closest Star—Our Sun

Warning: Never stare right at the sun.
You can damage your eyes if you do.

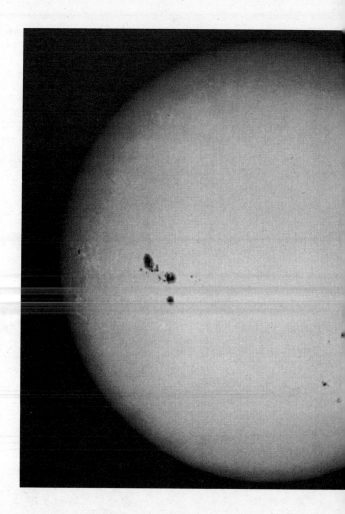

How close to Earth is our sun?

Our sun is about 93 million miles away from Earth. If you could travel to the sun at a speed of 25,000 miles per hour, it would take you more than five months to get there.

A lot of other stars are just as big, just as hot, and just as old as our sun. But because the sun is so close to Earth it is a very special star to us. Without it there would be no life on Earth. Our sun supplies the light and warmth and energy that makes our existence possible.

The dark spots on this photograph of the sun are sunspots—cooler, darker regions on the blazing sun.

YOUR WEIGHT ON THE SUN IS 28 TIMES YOUR EARTH WEIGHT!

Which is bigger, the sun or the earth?

The sun is much bigger than the earth. You would have to line up *109 Earths* to reach across the sun.

Because the sun is so big, its gravity is much stronger than Earth's gravity. You would weigh 28 *times* more on the sun than you do on Earth. If you could step on a scale on the sun, how much would you weigh?

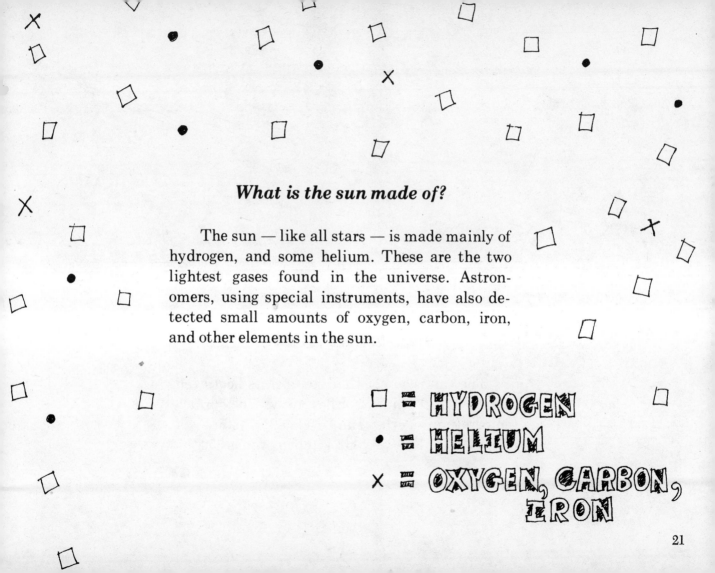

What is the sun made of?

The sun — like all stars — is made mainly of hydrogen, and some helium. These are the two lightest gases found in the universe. Astronomers, using special instruments, have also detected small amounts of oxygen, carbon, iron, and other elements in the sun.

□ = HYDROGEN

• = HELIUM

✗ = OXYGEN, CARBON, IRON

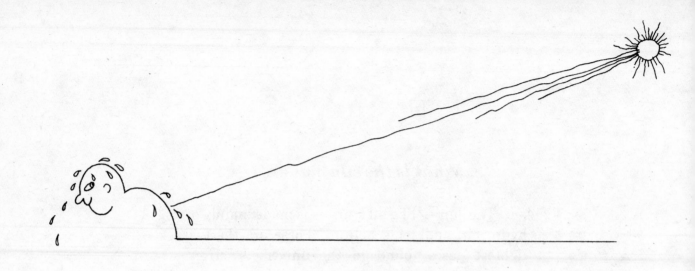

How hot is the sun?

The sun is so hot that you feel its heat even though it is 93 million miles away. The surface temperature of the sun — a yellow star — is about 10,000°F. A very hot kitchen oven is 550°F.

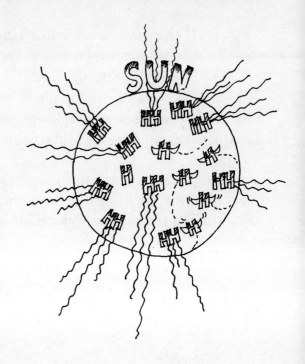

Why is the sun so hot and bright?

Nuclear fusion makes the sun (and other stars) hot and bright. Here's how it works:

Inside the sun, tiny particles of hydrogen are flying around, crashing into each other like buzzing bees in a jar. Each particle is a tiny nucleus of hydrogen. When the particles crash, they stick together, or fuse. A new particle is formed and energy — heat and light — is released.

Trillions and trillions of hydrogen particles are fusing all the time inside the sun. Energy builds up and pours out of the sun. This energy is radiation. We call it sunshine.

Will the sun ever stop shining?

Yes. But not for billions of years.

The sun was born about five billion years ago. It has been shining ever since. And astronomers say our sun is still only halfway through its life.

Many stars appear to be at least 10 billion years old. Our sun looks like these stars. It should keep shining for another five billion years before it dies.

What will happen when the sun dies?

After five billion years the sun will have used up most of its hydrogen. Then, astronomers think, the sun will start to get bigger. Its color will turn from yellow to red. It will become an old star called a *red giant*.

The red giant sun will make the earth very hot. Rocks will melt and oceans will evaporate. All living things on Earth will die.

Finally, the sun will collapse. It will shrink in size. Its surface will get very hot and white. It will become a small dying star called a *white dwarf*.

At the end of its life, the sun will stop shining. It will then be a lifeless black mass in space.

Finding a Planet

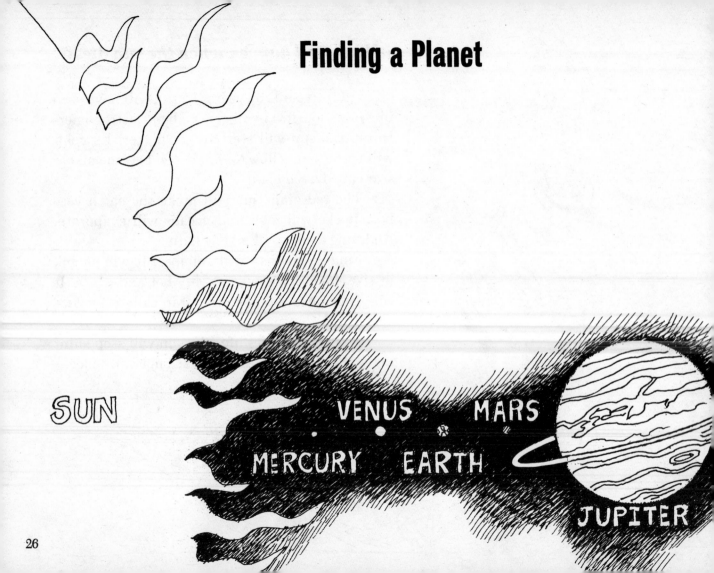

SUN

MERCURY
VENUS
EARTH
MARS
JUPITER

Which planets can you see in the sky?

You can see Venus, Mars, Jupiter, and Saturn at different times during the year.

Venus and Mars are the closest planets to Earth. Jupiter and Saturn are the biggest of all the planets.

The other planets — Mercury, Uranus, Neptune, and Pluto — are too small or too far away to be seen easily with your naked eye.

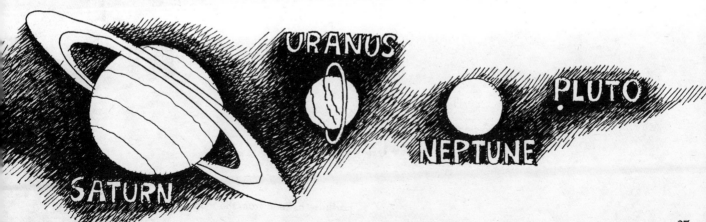

What makes the planets shine?

Planets act like giant mirrors in the sky. If you shine a flashlight at a mirror, light is reflected back to you. The sun shines light onto the planets. This light is reflected back out into space. It is this reflected sunlight that makes the planets shine in the sky.

If you could go out into space, you would see Earth shine the way all the other planets shine.

Earthrise as seen from the moon.

How can you find a planet in the sky?

Planets do not belong to groups the way stars seem to belong to constellations. In fact, the word planet comes from the Greek word meaning "wanderer."

Planets move in a path around the sun, and astronomers can figure out where and when the planets will appear in the sky. Most daily newspapers will tell you when and where planets will appear in the sky. If you want to find the planet Venus (which is sometimes called the Morning, or Evening Star) look up its position in the sky on the opposite page.

Morning Sky
(In the East *before* sunrise)

From mid-June 1980 to early April 1981
From late January 1982 to early November 1982
From late August 1983 to mid-June 1984
From early April 1985 to mid-January 1986
From early November 1986 to late August 1987
From mid-June 1988 to early April 1989

Evening Sky
(In the West *after* sunset)

From early April 1981 to late January 1982
From early November 1982 to late August 1983
From mid-June 1984 to early April 1985
From mid-January 1986 to early November 1986
From late August 1987 to mid-June 1988
From early April 1989 to mid-January 1990

Venus photographed from a spacecraft, 450,000 miles away.

Are there living things on other planets?

Maybe. The exciting search for living things on other planets began when the unmanned Viking Lander touched down on Mars on July 20, 1976. Scientists don't expect to find earthlike people on Mars. They are looking for living things so small they can only be seen through a microscope.

What will future space explorers find, millions of miles from planet Earth?

A dune field on Mars, photographed from the Viking Lander on August 3, 1976.

The Moon

What did the astronauts find on the moon?

The astronauts found no air or water on the moon. And in six Apollo trips, they never found any living thing on the moon.

They brought back **843** pounds of moon rock and soil for earth scientists to study in their laboratories. Scientists will be studying this material for years to come. They have found that some of the moon rocks are as old as 4 billion 600 million years.

ne of the astronauts of Apollo 15 and the Lunar
oving Vehicle on the moon in 1971.

What makes the moon shine?

The moon — like the planets — shines by reflecting sunlight. The moon is the biggest and brightest light in our nighttime sky because it is so close to Earth. It is only about 240,000 miles away.

Our moon is called a satellite of Earth because it revolves around our earth. Our planet has only one natural satellite. But there are many man-made satellites circling our earth. Some are weather information satellites, some are communications satellites relaying television programs and telephone calls around the world.

The moon on the 3rd, 5th, and 8th days after New Moon. At New Moon the moon is dark.

Why does the moon's appearance change?

Because the moon is going around the earth every month.

Half of the moon is always shining brightly in space, but the part we see changes as the moon moves in its orbit around Earth. The different shapes of the moon are called *phases*.

A New Moon occurs when the moon is between the sun and the earth.

The First Quarter (and Last Quarter) shines when the moon has gone ¼ (or ¾) of its way around Earth.

The Full Moon shines when the moon is on the opposite side of Earth from the sun.

The moon's phases repeat every 29½ days as it keeps orbiting Earth. Look for the different phases of the moon each month.

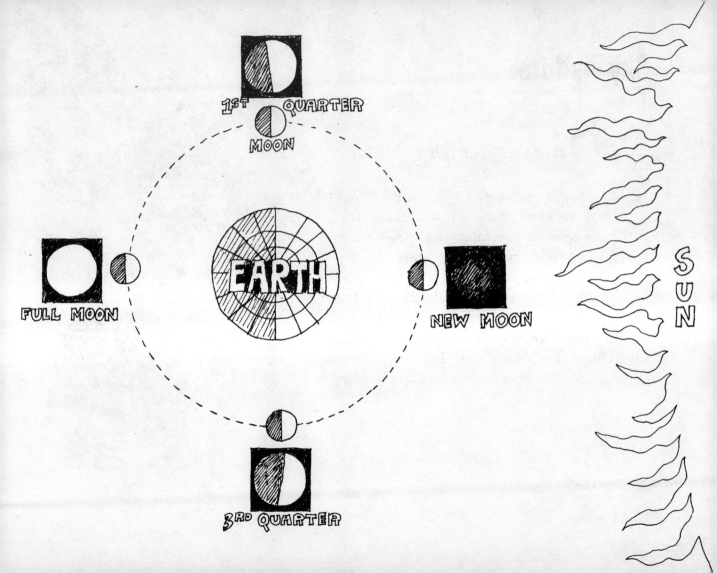

Sky Visitors

Did you ever wish on a star?

Some people say: "If you make a wish on a shooting star, your wish will come true." If you have tried it, you know that you have to be very quick to wish on a shooting star.

Shooting, or falling, stars aren't really stars at all. They are the streaks of light that can be seen when tiny particles from outer space burn up as they race down through Earth's atmosphere. They fall at speeds up to 45 miles per second.

Scientists call shooting stars *meteors*.

An iron meteorite, about 13 inches long and weighing
33 pounds, which fell in Nueva Leon, Mexico.

What is a meteorite?

A piece of stone or metal from outer space
that lands on earth is called a *meteorite.*

Hundreds of meteorites crash through
Earth's atmosphere every year. Most of them are
small and land in oceans or places where few people live. The largest meteorite ever found weighs
about 120,000 pounds. It is still in South-West
Africa, where it fell from the sky many years ago.

Meteorites are valuable. Recently a nine-
year-old girl was playing near her home in Con-
necticut when a small meteorite fell nearby. She
got $100 for sending it to scientists at the Univer-
sity of California at Los Angeles.

Halley's Comet photographed in 1910.

What is a comet?

A comet is a frozen ball of dust and gas traveling through space. Comets travel in orbits around the sun. When they come near the sun they reflect sunlight and begin to shine. Also, the wind and heat of the sun cause a long tail to form on a comet. The word comet means "long-haired."

When a comet leaves the sunlight and goes back out into space it stops shining.

Did you know that a comet could make you famous?

Every year about five new comets come into our sky. Most of them aren't bright enough to be seen without binoculars or a telescope. But many people spend long hours looking for new comets.

Why? Because each new comet is named after the person who discovers it. If you find a new comet, it will be named after you.

The most famous comet of all shines in our sky every 76 years. That's Halley's Comet. It's due back in 1986.

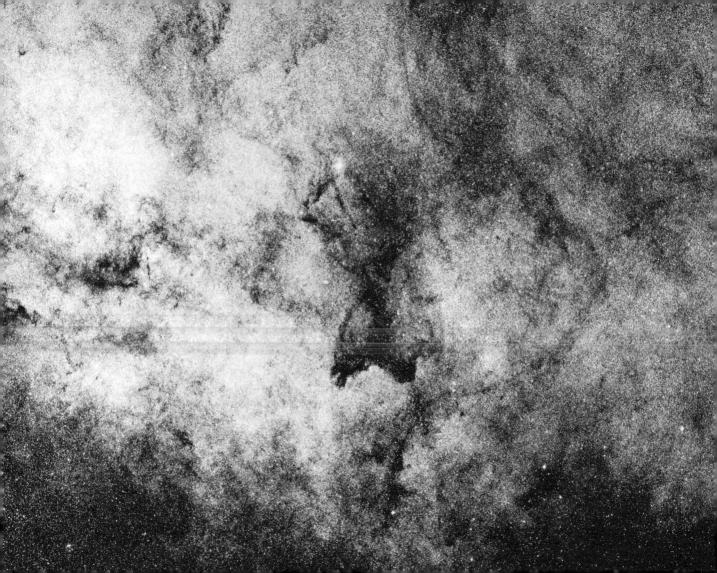

Exploring the Milky Way

What is the Milky Way?

The Milky Way is the cloudy band of light that you can see across the sky on a very clear dark night. It is easiest to observe in the summertime. The Milky Way got its name long ago because it looked like a milky trail in the sky. With binoculars or a telescope you can see that it is made up of an enormous number of stars. Such an enormous group of stars is called a *galaxy*.

Our sun and all the planets in our solar system and all the stars in our sky belong to the Milky Way Galaxy. The cloud of milky light you see in the night sky is a part of the Milky Way Galaxy.

A section of the Milky Way photographed through a large telescope.

What does the Milky Way Galaxy look like?

If you could go out into space and look down at our galaxy, you would see a bright spiral of glowing light — something like a giant pinwheel.

Our earth and our sun are out in one of the spiral arms of the Milky Way Galaxy.

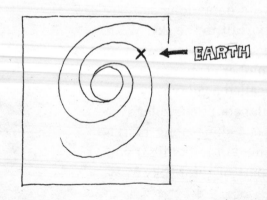

A spiral galaxy, similar to our own Milky Way, photographed through a large telescope.

If you could look at the Milky Way Galaxy from the side, it would look something like a phonograph record with a swollen label.

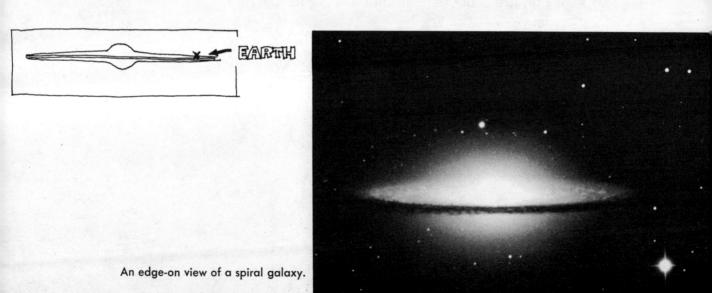

An edge-on view of a spiral galaxy.

How big is our galaxy?

The Milky Way Galaxy is about 100,000 light-years across. That is almost 600 thousand trillion miles! If you could ride on a light beam, it would take you 100,000 years to cross the Milky Way Galaxy.

Our solar system is racing around the center of our galaxy at about 560,000 mph. Yet it takes about 200 million years for our solar system to make just one trip around the center of our galaxy.

None of the stars in our galaxy has a really close neighbor. Each star is about five light-years away from its nearest neighbor. That's 30 trillion miles!

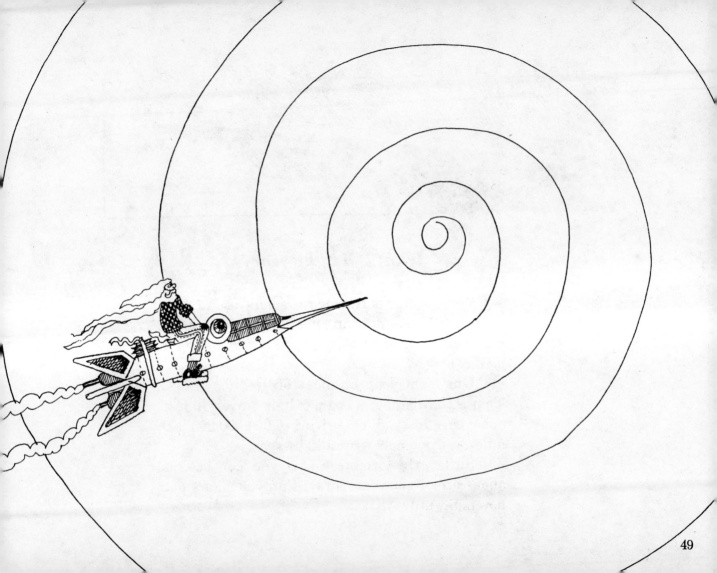

1 LIGHT YEAR = 6,000,000,000,000 MI

What is a light-year?

A light-year is the measurement used to describe vast distances in space. If you measured distance in space by miles, you'd be writing zeros all day long.

One light-year is about six trillion miles. That is the distance a beam of light travels in just one year. Instead of writing 6,000,000,000,000 miles, astronomers write 1 light-year.

Sirius, the brightest star you can see, is about nine light-years away. Can you figure out how many miles that is?

How can scientists study our huge galaxy?

By radio waves. Many objects in space send out strong radio waves. Luckily clouds don't stop radio waves from reaching Earth. Radio waves bring information about parts of our galaxy that we can't see — even with the biggest optical telescopes.

Dish-shaped receivers, called *radio telescopes*, collect radio waves from space. They are called radio *telescopes* because astronomers use them to "look" into space.

A radio telescope.

A Look Into Space

How far out into space can you see?

You can see very far out into space without using binoculars or a telescope. The most distant object ever visible to the naked eye is another galaxy out in the blackness of space — the Andromeda Galaxy. It is two million light-years away. That means that the light you see left the Andromeda Galaxy two million years ago!

The Andromeda Galaxy looks like a small white spot of light in the sky. It looks tiny because it is so far away. But it is bigger than our Milky Way Galaxy.

The Andromeda Galaxy.

How big is the universe?

The universe is still a mystery. We can see farther into space than anyone ever saw before, but there is a lot we don't know about our universe yet.

The biggest telescopes we have today are the radio telescopes. They can "see" out to puzzling objects called *quasars,* short for "quasi-stellar sources." Nobody knows what a quasar is, but astronomers do know that quasars send out a lot of light and powerful radio waves. The quasars seem to be the most distant objects we can see in our universe.

Astronomers have found a quasar that seems to be about 15 billion light-years away. That means that the universe is so big that it took a beam of light from that quasar at least 15 billion years to get to Earth.

A cluster of many galaxies far out in the univers photographed through the largest telescope in th United States, at the Hale Observatories in Californi

What is a nebula?

The word *nebula* comes from Latin and means cloud. A nebula is a cloud of gas and dust in space. Many nebulas have special names.

The Orion Nebula is a cloud in which new stars are being born. The Crab Nebula is the remains of a gigantic star that was seen exploding in the year 1054 A.D.

Sometimes nebulas block out starlight making strange dark patterns in space. One such cloud looks like a giant horse's head. Astronomers call it the Horsehead Nebula. You would need binoculars or a telescope to see these famous nebulas clearly.

The Great Nebula in Orion.

The Horsehead Nebula.

The Crab Nebula.

Are there any creatures living someplace out in space?

The chances are good that there are. There are billions of galaxies in space. Each of them has billions and billions of stars inside. Many of those stars are probably like our sun. So the chances are good that some of those stars have a planet like Earth — with a climate that is comfortable for life.

Astronomers have found the basic chemicals of life out in space. Now they're looking for another star with a planet, like our sun-and-earth system. If they find one, maybe they'll find other living creatures as well.

You and the Stars

How can you use the stars?

The stars can help you tell direction. One star always shines from the same place in the sky. It shines in the north all night long, every night of the year. This star is called the North Star (Polaris).

Two stars in the bowl of the Big Dipper always point to the North Star.

If you face the North Star, then you know that North is ahead of you, South is at your back, East is on your right, and West is on your left.

NORTH STAR

What are some questions that don't have any answers yet?

Astronomers have found out many of the secrets of the universe. But there are many questions that nobody can answer yet. For instance:

What do the other planets look like close up?
What *are* the puzzling quasars?
Are there intelligent creatures somewhere out in the universe trying to talk to us on earth?

There are many more star mysteries left to solve. Will you be an astronomer detective one day?

The 200-inch Hale telescope—the largest in the United States—with the shutter open.

How can you find out more about the stars?

1. Go to a planetarium. Many cities have planetariums. There you can see star shows on a big dome that looks just like the real sky. Astronomers at the planetarium can help you find out more about stars.

2. Look at stars through a big telescope. Observatories, museums, planetariums, and universities often let people look through their telescopes. Call to find out when the telescopes are open for public viewing.

3. Go to your public library. You'll find astronomy books and magazines with star maps and more information about the stars.

4. Check your daily newspaper. It will tell you the time the sun, the moon, and the planets rise and set each day. It will also tell you when the different phases of the moon will occur.

5. Join an amateur astronomers' club. People of all ages form clubs to look at the stars and talk about what they have seen. Or start your own club.

6. Study the stars each night. That way the sky will become as familiar to you as the streets or roads in your own neighborhood.